The poems themselves are archives, of the body, of place, of the body's gestures and movings through the city of these poems. The images are electric with worry and wonder, memory and possibility, and through it all, love.
—Natalie Diaz judge of the Charlotte Mew Prize

"What does courage mean anymore?" asks the speaker in Freesia McKee's *How Distant the City*, a question that pulses through the nuanced body of this book to its profound extremities. "She would fly home more, but TSA never knows who to get to do the pat-down," comes one moment of revelation. "You realized your pain isn't the only pain/ worth knowing," comes another. *How Distant the City* is a courageous and arresting debut.
—Julie Marie Wade author of *When I Was Straight* and *SIX: Poems*

Freesia McKee's *How Distant the City* is a city of questions, asking us to account for how we pay attention to our small wild moments in a time made strange by war. This poet pushes us to keep circling around what most would pass by to mark our stains on each page, to turn our ears to notice who has gone by and who has gone missing.
—Ching-In Chen author of *The Heart's Traffic* and *recombinant*

Freesia McKee's debut chapbook, *How Distant the City*, illuminates geographical, emotional and psychic spaces to expose the alienation and displacement we create when we substitute apathy and avoidance for empathy and connection. This collection shines most brilliantly in poems that connect the quotidian to the remarkable, traversing with linguistic adroitness through representations of loss, rape, racial injustice, murder and commonplace acts such as getting a haircut or setting a Thanksgiving table. In the juxtaposition of everyday acts to acts of terror, McKee draws attention to the dialectics of the self's most private desires, struggles and traumas with those of the displaced and terrorized "others" in our villages, in our hearts, in our local and national news, and in our global community. McKee boldly makes connections across differences with a poetic fluency that is vibrant, honest, inspiring and chock-full of integrity.
—Donna Aza Weir-Soley author of *First Rain, Eroticism, Spirituality and Resistance in Black Women's Writings, The Woman Who Knew* and co-editor of *Caribbean Erotic*

How Distant the City

How Distant the City

Freesia McKee

HEADMISTRESS PRESS

ISBN-13: 978-0998761022
ISBN-10: 0998761028

Cover art © Freesia McKee, *Oak Leaf Trail,* 2016
Back cover photo of Freesia McKee © Gloria Martinez, 2015
Cover & book design by Mary Meriam

PUBLISHER
Headmistress Press
60 Shipview Lane
Sequim, WA 98382
Telephone: 917-428-8312
Email: headmistresspress@gmail.com
Website: headmistresspress.blogspot.com

Contents

Meanwhile

Meanwhile, you are writing poetry about outer space.
Meanwhile, you forgot it even happened.
Meanwhile, you had such a nice Thanksgiving talking
about table decorations.
Meanwhile, you are getting your hair cut.

Meanwhile, you "agree to disagree."
Meanwhile, you breeze through security, read a book
just for fun, watch tv, play a video game with a gun.
Meanwhile, you sleep well.

Once in a while, you think about war zones
and what it might feel like to walk past a body.

Meanwhile, you do yoga.
Meanwhile, you eat a sandwich.
Meanwhile, you "treat yourself."
Meanwhile, you drive past a city.

Meanwhile, you take a plane ride to Washington. Two white
boys sit next to you talking about students who are mugged
on their campus. The school distributes security reports profiling
the suspects. Muggers always look the same, the boys agree.

Meanwhile, you "don't see color."
Meanwhile, you "earned every penny."
Meanwhile, "he was no angel."

He is now.

Meanwhile, you stroll without pain.
Meanwhile, you grip your iced tea.
Meanwhile, your narrowest scope.

Meanwhile, you're—

Marie Sends Her Regards and Memories

handwritten letters her mother threw out, photographs of great-
aunt Marie wearing chaps and waders. an athlete, a cowgirl, a
car across the state. the small apartment of two very best friends.
a painter, a writer, or did she straighten out. great-aunt Marie:
a church lady, a mother. she poured coffee all day. she stayed
awake. she drank, she sang, she always smiled. her lips were tight;
she never talked. rigid, bent, unbought. Marie's picture cradled.
Marie, who thought she might be. graceful, discerning Marie
of the cardboard figure. she outwit you. could be. her, sharp as
a new metal ruler. now that she is gone, all I can say of Marie is
what other people thought. far currency and furrow. girl in the
stream. a fisher, a football. the quiet Maries of other times and
persuasions. the Marie descended. might have been your teacher,
your butcher, your first girlfriend.

Small Lungs

In the kitchen
I chopped carrots and the radio talked

about the killings. I felt a wall building
inside. I cut my thumb

by accident. I told you how my cousin shot
a squirrel out of a tree, throwing the warm

body into the woods. The squirrel who climbed
up near his house.

The first time I danced with you,
a woman in the band played a trombone.

What does courage mean anymore?
You held my hand in the parking lot

in a town we didn't know. I drove down
to Pride the summer of Orlando. I told you

about the men I've known with loaded
guns. Fireworks blazed near the edge

of land. Past them, we could see
oil rigs. You said *think about how much*

we've been through since then, all of us.
Why did my cousin kill that squirrel? What image

makes you cry every time you see it?
The cut thumb pulsing, the clogged sink

drain. A photograph of people lined
up around the block to give blood.

We found a rabbit the size of a small bar of soap
in the parking lot. We held her and could feel

her pulse, her voice surprising. We are not
moving to Orlando, but we felt the loud

heart in such a small body, thumbing
repeatedly like missed calls. One of the first nights

you came over, you carried lumber
up the stairs to make a bookshelf.

Where do two women go to dance together?
We slept upstairs on mats in an empty

room. A woman in the band played
the trombone. We named the rabbit

Violet. The flap of skin healed.
The sound of the gun stopped

echoing after the small animal fell.
I drove home to you that night.

Out of the Museum

You realized your pain isn't the only pain
worth knowing

after a slick rock flipped

one hundred times in your pocket
and landed on heads.

How far did you travel

to meet that medium: your hands
in the clay of your making?

Compressed so hot, change
was the only thing you could see, fiery planet
born into a language turned by a thousand
pairs of patient hands.

in California

in the alley Where feral cats live
I saw a raccoon creeping

in the garbage Survivor Wish I
could feel anger sound low
in the chest to act on
identifying with

the smallest creatures
Where feral cats live
a person is a metaphor

Waking curled like sick kittens
towards the head of a sheet We run
from the silent ones They say

thousands of feral cats live in this city
but how many guns in this building
and how many guns in this street where feral cats live

and how many guns add up to a pixelated / adolescence
and how many guns add up to narcissistic / heroism

Maybe he felt it was the way to—
How many shots to make—
Did he think that people would—

There is no cat who hates herself that much
What does she think when she hears people screaming
in our alley or in the morning
or during lunchtime or in a beach town

This True Question

The darkness is what gets me
A wild and rigid gain
My smothered lawn My scissors
A real woman Mythic

My hard said: wait
You are moving through
and I will always be a traitor
My stomach is a darkness

and every woman has her dragon
her cow her big and every woman has her pig
stomach punctured
Isn't every woman at least

a little this way? Working three
times through the sitting room
A spread out bag gone missing
A little house within

Her back half snapped
a given
An ant under a
paper

What do I want to say to her?
My turtle's hands are touching
Her half her dark her bailiwick
Her wheelhouse her bag her fiction

She looms near my head my covers
She weaves myself my shoulders
I hide my keys inside the
flowerpot Gold sticks to my coat

My body boards the red line with
An ache's relentless badger

Poem for Dorothy Allison

I am chalk, a winter
splotch on this Midwestern beach.
Days swing by. We fly into the open
lake. She is my unblurry memory,
unintended, heaped on a plate.

She smashes the head of a song
against a lowered door.

The brunt of its force, stone
like a monument in my stomach.
We print our mistakes
defiant. Every movement
we make stains on the page.

Transit Status

I dreamed that I used my smaller hands to put out
a fire in a crib A dollhouse
I dreamed that I burned my hands but said it was okay
like All my time in Seattle alone visiting

the lesbian bar alone in Chicago
visiting the lesbian bar alone What was I searching for?
Another life, I guess

Everyone on their digital in the metal box
passing by I turn away from the rain
Waiting for another bus in these legs I sewed up to look

more modern and There you are
at the axis The words slicking off me
I wanna spread out here I wanna write the theory

where we are at the bus stop where the trash bag
broke and no one is watching and I am not afraid
The legs of my jeans rusty from your basement floor
I notice before you drive away

She Asks If You're Leaving

Thinking about the girl girl
At the waterpark On this train
On my way home not home
Fiberglass lily pads float in the pool with chains
running to the bottom
A heron appears in the corner of the train's
window The moon grows
and I think about the good girl girl
in a city
or between
two cities
Sliding through the Cumberland
goggles blurry in my backpack
I am not returning home I think but
I cannot swim or pass the swimming test
My shirt pulls tight from train station
to bus station Bad fit but No one knows me here
not the man who stares or the teenagers
I follow all the way to the lake
as they laugh and carry a box
of donuts for someone's birthday
I am like a dog who follows
I can't swim well but I paddle
Walking through Chicago
I think *I could do anything here*
Which is to say that every other man I meet
has made a film and moved somewhere
My imaginary brothers pass the tests
*I will go home now because my stomach
hurts* I say *I have asthma*

and I think about the girl girl I think
about the girl girl
girl girl I am not returning home I am
returning home not home
A trained hand slides the train through wetlands
Coyote asks *Are you leaving*
or returning? I say both

.

An Icy Stop

Flying down the gorge You met her
Jealousy proverb in a store
window Took All the garbage
meadows The trash I may be into
Telling Very
your thigh your tie dye your
tie around your next I am
a dog who digs
everywhere Couldn't unstick
that unearthed feeling Burrowing
Drawn out and foreshadowed
Caught up in the
shallow ditch Garbage trucks
echo The raccoon of the alley
Your trained eye for plant ID Your
keen a train Your light box on empty shade
My knee always A mouse
who milks a cow or goat but not
a Chicken melts and melts and like an Icy
strip someone placed in the park And
maybe even at the table
I riff on you

Haircuts

Mostly, I am thinking about haircuts. Loans and phone bills, the two pounds I gained this month, where I can buy new pants like the tight pair on a woman standing in front of me. I am getting coffee. In America. What the president said. I heard him. I read a book about travel. I wrote a poem. This morning, I turned on the radio as they talked about. I remember the French word for "rape" from a high school class. But I am not thinking about. What I heard this morning.

A journalist. A woman. A hundred men. Tahrir Square. Raped with their hands. Their male hands. Like crowd surfing. *The first big concert I went to we were 15 someone tried to? Unhook her bra? My friend at the concert wanted to crowd surf she kept trying to? Climb on the stage, ripped jeans and makeup?*

A cloth is more powerful than a woman. Or a cloth makes a woman powerful. Or a cloth makes a woman realize her power. I heard that someone in a chador pulled the journalist from the crowd, from the concert of hands. Imagine points of contact, finally, woman to woman. The sound of a chador sinking over her head.

Rape. A human shield and a human gun. Rape. Their big male hands. Rape. Getting home. Remember three men in a subway, a snarl. Rape. But I am not thinking about. What? Rape. I am not thinking about. I am trying to get skinny. I am drinking my coffee. A veiled escape at the next stop. A woman, a woman. No, I am not thinking about. Cloth. *I kind of want the same haircut I got last time? Shorter sideburns and more dramatic bangs?* Rape. War tools. Scheduling the appointment for my hair as the radio drones.

Date Grape

"Brewer responds to protests about offensive beer name"
—*Milwaukee Journal Sentinel,* December 7, 2016

What if I took the worst thing
that's happened to you
and joked about it

and joked about it
Using you as both
ammunition and target

Puckered up
shut down
What if I pit you

against yourself
Only a
joke Stoked to win

the same old contests
If I add some sour
to the sweetness

how does it taste?

Concord seedless
purple like a bruise
wrinkled fruit

The bitterest grape
the stapled shut lip
All the bars I've jumped

      over sleeping in anger
      holding
      that sour grape

      date rape

Poem for Ashraf Fayadh

19 poets in one room eat
beans and rice We talk

about writing the whole summer Who has
a new book

out How it's been received
Perhaps this is the way

poets in any country speak We try to remember
if they've reduced your sentence

What can 19 quiet people do
from all the way out here?

The difference
between 800 and 400 lashes

and the distance between 400 and
zero These mathematics you already know

We take a lot of time to measure
the circumference shoulder-to-shoulder

speaking with each other
about who's in power

Hot Chick

A supervisor says
you are a "hot chick,
just like the others."
"Just pretend that
he said *you go girl,*"
a female boss says
when you finally complain.
You think: you wouldn't have
taken the job to be hot.
A year later, you hear
a woman say she has never
been employed without harassment.
You know
where she works and still,
you say nothing.
Later, you think every day
of that job, digging trenches
in the sun with the women
beside you.
A deep fold of seeds
sits angry in your palm,
waiting in silence for some water
to bloom.

The Union

Somewhere a poet
starts building a room. Two cats sunbathe
in the scrappy old yard where the poet has
taken her axe to the logs. Each hour splits

as the poet hones her blade.
The cats call when the poet takes rest on a stump.
Why don't you use any nails? they say.
Do you even know how to hew a raw trunk?

Each time the poet splits herself here,
the yard's edge opens to the dark
of the room.

The poet accepts the only choice. The lazy cats run away.

Have you built a dark space without nails or blueprints?
Have you abandoned the lot that they told you to build?
What is as irresistible as the pull of a stump?

The poet sits down alone. The poet pays her dues.

in North Carolina

It's really short, her mother says. A new cut. She buys a knit cap
at the truck stop. In a borrowed car, she hits an opossum. The
thunk in the fastest lane. The cry. She sees a dead bear on the
switchbacks driving to Charlotte. She would fly home more,
but TSA never knows who to get to do the pat-down. There's a
bible verse printed on her milkshake's Styrofoam cup. Strawberry
shortcake. Key lime pie. Coconut cream. Wedding cake.

A Standing Still

fox danced between
the very still waters headed north
past geese and white-beaked
birds leaving V's in the water, far

from the cocker spaniel five minutes
before or lighted towers
brightening our left sides as we risky
walked beneath darker skies

I felt the opaque absence of fear for her
closer billowed rough tail and dark mimicking rings
so I stood taller, still, and watched as long
and large fox danced her solitary way
through a city built despite her

These Are the Questions

these are the questions i wo-
nder because even the grown-up
men ask you to cook dinner
tuna casserole starts with a roux
but bugs got into the flour
when your grandmother died and
cleaning the bin means you
would need arms longer than you
have at the moment so
you close that option, walk
to the store, carry your pounds
back, long-handled spoon drawing
memories out with the butter
finding the answer: you are
the last woman to cook in this house
before you are even a woman

Home

The want for you
screams loud like a trumpet,
like a prairie wind.
Inside my room, windows
chain and clank
and the record spins on.
You're like a single
book I read over and over
again. I turn the page
on its brass elbow
and your words sing through
all these walls.

on 47th Street

that night of what some would
call riots   helicopters circling

we got home and walked the dog
in the middle of the night

when I heard about the killing
I lit a stick of incense
took five steps across the floor

when someone dies abruptly
who and what absorbs the sound?

there was a war today
here and here
no one can see outside

the windows of most prisons I hear
the cells face inward I hear
several streets over

the sound
a rash of new shots

The Most Beautiful Yard in Milwaukee Award

when my mother finally told me why
she had stopped letting me visit your house,

she said, *you know, freesia,*
their father molested them,

and i got scared of how your secrets stacked up
like the little pieces of metal in your middle

school desk, the geometry of your box
turtle on its back.

i know your mother burned photographs
in the backyard, left the apartment

to spend nights with gargoyles
in the garden, and

it was a long drive
from you on the north side back

to my house on the south. you said your
mother bought reptiles, another cat, three dogs

in one year. the littlest one looked just like mine
but she had a fit in your fenced yard and died.

you said your parents made you cut
the whole yard with a shears after that.

maybe i shouldn't pull up
these questions now,

it seems that we are stacked
like stones. but what if i had known

when you sharpened
paper clips and cut dirt

that white cats would only leave dander

like ashes.

Pale Risks

if it wasn't so easy to be an activist through twitter
if the protest didn't happen during the football game
let me explain
if i had skin in the game
more time
if it was Selma
if my daughter's life was
or my son
i'm about to leave this city for good
right now i'm eating breakfast
really busy
i work full-time and no one's asked me
directly
maybe when i get another job
but i sign petitions
vote in every election
i protest through my art
if i was younger and more energetic
if i had less to lose   more to lose
when i'm older
the courts will decide
don't break the laws
wait
don't alienate people
like me   who make laws
pick grand juries
what do you mean you can't wait

if this is my last message

for Aleppo

if danger crescendos
like a heating tea kettle

jaw of a broken jar
open as the mouth of the moon

if I die
still young

remember that I died
as people have always
died

as you lie

listening

do not remember me for
this last message

remember the song I sang

if you sleep through
what we lived for as it burns

think about my smoke

how when it touched your skin
you turned away

How Distant the City

"Six businesses burn in Milwaukee unrest"
—*Milwaukee Journal Sentinel,* August 14, 2016

when we decided
to fume quietly
To think of you
as a watered gesture
a drive
a storm too high to touch
Lightening
was a fact
The targets of death
Our neighbors
never truly random
How distant the city
The sky
billowed and struck
Some of us pretended
the wet ground
dry
When the world watched
little changed
All that burned
was a candle

About the Author

Freesia McKee is a poet, writer, performance artist, and radio host from Milwaukee. She creates work about power, gender, and apathy. Freesia's words have appeared in *Lavender Review, cream city review, Painted Bride Quarterly, Gertrude, The Feminist Wire, Huffington Post, Political Punch: Contemporary Poems on the Politics of Identity*, and other websites, magazines, and anthologies. She has performed and taught in bookstores, prisons, classrooms, summer camps, arts groups, and youth programs.

In the wake of the 2016 election, Freesia self-published a series of post-election poems called *For the Immediate Aftermath* and a community anthology *Permeable to the Year* co-curated with Anja Notanja Sieger. Freesia and Anja also co-hosted 57 weekly episodes of "The Subtle Forces," an improvisational literary morning show on Riverwest Radio in Milwaukee.

Freesia has curated and MC'd poetry readings and open mics to support International Women's Day, Writers Resist, Black & Pink, the Standing Rock Water Protectors, Woodland Pattern Poetry Center, and other groups and causes. With five other artists, she participated in Grin City Collective's "Map of Things No Longer Here" collaborative residency in Grinnell, Iowa. Her group examined the telephone as historian and history-teller. They published a usable "phone book of special skills," built a phone booth facsimile into which participants brought their own cell phones, and installed the "Museum of the Obsolete."

In 2017, Freesia moved from Milwaukee to North Miami to pursue an MFA in poetry at Florida International University. She has a degree in Gender & Women's Studies from Warren Wilson College. Freesia is available for readings, workshops, residencies, curatorial and mentoring opportunities, and literary community-building. Learn more about Freesia's work at FreesiaMcKee.wordpress.com

Acknowledgments

CALYX (Vol. 30:3, Summer/Fall 2018): "Transit Status"

Eat Local :: Read Local: "Poem for Ashraf Fayadh"

Ishaan Literary Review: "The Most Beautiful Yard in Milwaukee Award"

Lavender Review: "Home"

New Verse News: "if this is my last message"

Peal: "these are the questions"

Political Punch: Contemporary Poems on the Politics of Identity: "Haircuts," "The Most Beautiful Yard in Milwaukee Award"

Return to the Gathering Place of the Waters: Milwaukee Poets in 2017: "on 47th Street"

The Feminist Wire: "Date Grape"

The Wanderer: "An Icy Stop"

Visitant (formerly PDXX Collective): "Out of the Museum," "in California," "Poem for Dorothy Allison," "Hot Chick," "A Standing Still," "Pale Risks"

Woodland Pattern Blog: "The Union"

Headmistress Press Books

Lovely - Lesléa Newman
Teeth & Teeth - Robin Reagler
How Distant the City - Freesia McKee
Shopgirls - Marissa Higgins
Riddle - Diane Fortney
When She Woke She Was an Open Field - Hilary Brown
God With Us - Amy Lauren
A Crown of Violets - Renée Vivien tr. Samantha Pious
Fireworks in the Graveyard - Joy Ladin
Social Dance - Carolyn Boll
The Force of Gratitude - Janice Gould
Spine - Sarah Caulfield
Diatribe from the Library - Farrell Greenwald Brenner
Blind Girl Grunt - Constance Merritt
Acid and Tender - Jen Rouse
Beautiful Machinery - Wendy DeGroat
Odd Mercy - Gail Thomas
The Great Scissor Hunt - Jessica K. Hylton
A Bracelet of Honeybees - Lynn Strongin
Whirlwind @ Lesbos - Risa Denenberg
The Body's Alphabet - Ann Tweedy
First name Barbie last name Doll - Maureen Bocka
Heaven to Me - Abe Louise Young
Sticky - Carter Steinmann
Tiger Laughs When You Push - Ruth Lehrer
Night Ringing - Laura Foley
Paper Cranes - Dinah Dietrich
On Loving a Saudi Girl - Carina Yun
The Burn Poems - Lynn Strongin
I Carry My Mother - Lesléa Newman
Distant Music - Joan Annsfire
The Awful Suicidal Swans - Flower Conroy
Joy Street - Laura Foley
Chiaroscuro Kisses - G.L. Morrison
The Lillian Trilogy - Mary Meriam
Lady of the Moon - Amy Lowell, Lillian Faderman, Mary Meriam
Irresistible Sonnets - ed. Mary Meriam
Lavender Review - ed. Mary Meriam

9 780998 761022